YOU'VE GOT TO BE KIDDING, SNOOPY!

by CHARLES M. SCHULZ

Selected cartoons from
SPEAK SOFTLY AND CARRY A BEAGLE, Vol. 1

FAWCETT CREST • NEW YORK

YOU'VE GOT TO BE KIDDING, SNOOPY!

This book, prepared especially for Fawcett Crest Books, a unit of CBS Publications, the Consumer Publishing Division of CBS Inc., comprises the first part of *SPEAK SOFTLY, AND CARRY A BEAGLE* and is reprinted by arrangement with Holt, Rinehart and Winston, Inc.

ISBN: 0-449-23453-3

Printed in the United States of America

12   11   10   9   8   7   6   5   4   3

YOU'VE GOT TO BE KIDDING, SNOOPY!

FIRST YOU SWOOP IN ALL THE I'S....THEN YOU POP IN ALL THE DOTS....

IF THEY COME OUT EVEN, THAT'S GOOD PENMANSHIP!

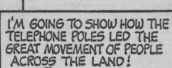

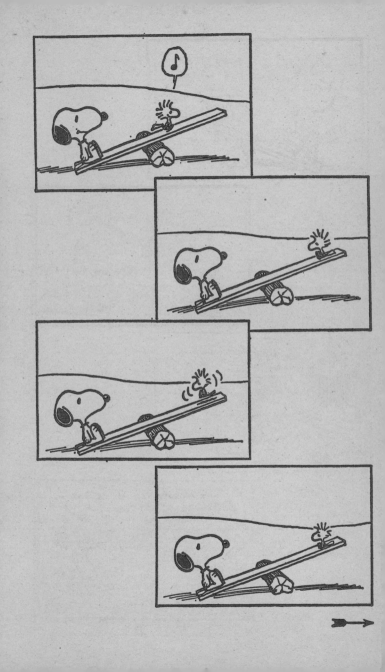

Dear Contributor,

We think your new story is magnificent.

We want to print it in our next issue, and will pay you One Thousand dollars.

P.S. April Fool!

Dutch Waltz, the famous skater, was worried.

His skating partner, Chil Blain, was in love.

While playing a show in Denver, she had become involved with a cowboy named Martin Gale.

THE STORY ISN'T MUCH, BUT THE NAMES ARE GREAT!

Immediately after he won the golf tournament, he was interviewed on TV.

"This is the most exciting moment of my life!" he said.

"I saw you on TV," said his wife. "I thought the day we got married was the most exciting moment of your life."

In his next tournament, he failed to make the cut.

Joe Anthro was an authority on Egyptian and Babylonian culture.

His greatest accomplishment, however, was his famous work on the Throat culture.

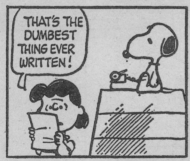

THAT'S THE DUMBEST THING EVER WRITTEN!

ANOTHER FIRST!

HI, CHUCK... IT'S BEEN KIND OF A LONG TIME, HUH?

YEAH, I'M BACK IN SCHOOL AGAIN...HOW'S SNOOPY'S DOG HOUSE? THAT SURE WAS EMBARRASSING...I HAD NO IDEA·HE WAS A BEAGLE...

I USED TO THINK HE WAS JUST A FUNNY-LOOKING KID WITH A BIG NOSE...THAT'S WHY I HAVEN'T CALLED YOU, I GUESS....

LET'S JUST SAY MY PRIDE HAD THE FLU, OKAY, CHUCK?

➤

WE'RE THE HOME TEAM, CHUCK, SO YOU GUYS BAT FIRST, AND WE'LL TAKE THE FIELD.

OKAY, SNOOPY, YOU'RE OUR LEAD-OFF BATTER...LET'S START THINGS OFF BIG...

BUT LOOK OUT FOR PEPPERMINT PATTY...SHE'S A GOOD PITCHER!

HERE WE GO! THE FIRST PITCH OF THE SEASON! I LOVE BASEBALL!

BONK!!

Gentlemen,
I am submitting a
story to your magazine
for consideration.

I have been a subscriber
to your magazine for
many years.

If you don't publish my
story, I am going to
cancel my subscription.

So there, too!

History Report;
Ancient Greece

Ancient Greece was
ahead of its time,
and before our time.

They had no TV,
but they had lots
of philosophers.

I, personally, would
not want to sit all
evening watching
a philosopher.

"THERE'S NO REASON FOR YOU TO KEEP COMING BACK TO THE NEST ON MOTHER'S DAY...THAT'S NOT THE WAY WE BIRDS DO THINGS!"

"ONCE YOU'VE LEFT, LITTLE BIRD, THAT'S IT! YOU CAN'T GO HOME AGAIN! SO FLY AWAY! DON'T LOOK BACK! THE WORLD IS YOURS!"

* SIGH *

I MUST ADMIT SHE'S A PRETTY SHARP MOTHER!

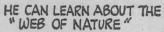

WELL, WHAT DOES A GOOD BEAGLE SCOUT DO WHEN HE'S LOST? ACTUALLY, HE HAS TWO CHOICES...

HE CAN PANIC, OR HE CAN CALMLY TAKE OUT HIS MAP AND COMPASS, AND CALMLY FIND HIS WAY BACK HOME...

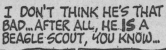

WELL, I'M GLAD TO SEE YOU'RE BACK

THANK YOU

BUT WHAT A DISASTER! YOU DISGRACED THE NAME OF "BEAGLE SCOUT"!

IMAGINE! GETTING LOST, AND THEN BEING RESCUED BY A GIRL SCOUT SELLING COOKIES!

THEY WERE GOOD COOKIES!

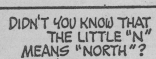

Dear Little Girl Scout,

Thank you for rescuing me when I was lost in the wilderness.

I hope I will see you again some day. Maybe you could come to my house for milk and cookies.

You bring the cookies.

Kitten Kaboodle was a lazy cat. Actually, all cats are lazy.

Kitten Kaboodle was also ugly, stupid and completely useless.

But, let's face it, aren't all cats ugly, stupid and completely useless?

I LOVE WRITING ANTI-CAT STORIES!

And so, once again, Kitten Kaboodle had to admit she had been outsmarted by a dog.

An ordinary dog at that.

DO YOU THINK THERE'S A MARKET FOR ANTI-CAT STORIES?

"PLAYBEAGLE" HAS BOUGHT THE WHOLE SERIES!

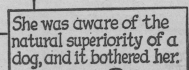

After that, Kitten Kaboodle never again tried to match wits with a dog.

DO YOU THINK YOUR ANTI-CAT STORIES WILL EVER BE MADE INTO A TELEVISION SERIES?

I EXPECT TO HEAR FROM ALL THREE NETWORKS... CBS, NBC AND ABC...

COLUMBIA BEAGLE SYSTEM, NATIONAL BEAGLE COMPANY AND THE AMERICAN BEAGLE COMPANY!

POW!

LOOK, CHARLIE BROWN...
I CAUGHT YOUR SHOE!

MAYBE I SHOULD PITCH MY SHOE INSTEAD OF THE BALL..

THAT'S A GOOD IDEA..GIVE 'EM THE OL' KNUCKLE SHOE!

LOOK, CHARLIE BROWN, MY APPLICATION NOT TO GO TO CAMP WAS ACCEPTED!

YOU, TOO?

BOY, WHAT A RELIEF! NO SUMMER CAMP!

"WE HAVE ESCAPED AS A BIRD FROM THE SNARE OF THE FOWLERS; THE SNARE IS BROKEN, AND WE HAVE ESCAPED!"..... KING DAVID, PSALM ONE HUNDRED TWENTY-FOUR'

I NEVER REALIZED THAT KING DAVID WORRIED ABOUT GOING TO CAMP...

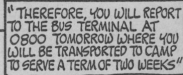

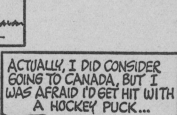